THE HISTORIC FORT WAYNE
EMBASSY THEATRE

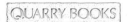

AN IMPRINT OF

Indiana University Press
Bloomington & Indianapolis

THE HISTORIC FORT WAYNE
EMBASSY THEATRE

Dyne L. Pfeffenberger

with contributions by
Marlyn E. Koons and Kathleen E. Skiba

Facing page. Robert I. Goldstine, March 9, 1916–June 20, 2001.
Embassy Theatre Foundation archives

This book is a publication of

Quarry Books
an imprint of

Indiana University Press
601 North Morton Street
Bloomington, IN 47404-3797 USA

http://iupress.indiana.edu

Telephone orders	800-842-6796
Fax orders	812-855-7931
Orders by e-mail	iuporder@indiana.edu

The paper used in this publication meets the minimum require-
ments of American National Standard for Information Sciences—
Permanence of Paper for Printed Library Materials, ANSI
Z39.48-1984.

Manufactured in China

Library of Congress Cataloging-in-Publication Data

Pfeffenberger, Dyne L.
  The historic Fort Wayne Embassy Theatre / Dyne L. Pfeffenberger;
with contributions by Marlyn E. Koons and Kathleen E. Skiba.
    p. cm.
  ISBN 978-0-253-31369-0 (cloth : alk. paper) 1. Embassy Theatre
(Fort Wayne, Ind.) 2. Historic buildings—Conservation and
restoration—Indiana—Fort Wayne. 3. Motion picture theaters—
Conservation and restoration—Indiana—Fort Wayne. 4. Fort
Wayne (Ind.)—Buildings, structures, etc. I. Koons, Marlyn E. II.
Skiba, Kathleen E. III. Title.
  NA6846.U62F677 2009
  725'.8220977274—dc22

                                        2008038719

1 2 3 4 5 14 13 12 11 10 09

This book is dedicated to the memory of

Bob Goldstine,

whose foresight, perseverance, and
leadership preserved and
enhanced a community treasure,
the Embassy Theatre.

CONTENTS

ACKNOWLEDGMENTS

This book would have been extremely difficult if not impossible to complete were it not for the assistance and encouragement so generously given by many talented and kind people. The variety of their contributions ranges from creative ideas, exceptional memories, and sophisticated technical assistance to superb photography, keen artistic sensitivity, and, yes, even funding. To each of you, my sincere thanks and profound appreciation.

Dyne L. Pfeffenberger

Harvey Cocks Jr.	*Lori Lobsiger*	*Bob Nickerson*
Roger Crawford	*Ginny Maloley*	*Kelly Updike*
John Foell	*Nellie Maloley*	*Steve Vorderman*
Steve Linsenmayer	*Alan Nauts*	*Dana Wichern*

CHRONOLOGY

May 14, 1928	Grand opening, Emboyd Theatre
May 24, 1928	Indiana Hotel opens for business
1932	Fort Wayne natives Olsen and Johnson produce *Hellzapoppin* at Emboyd Theatre
Early 1935	W. Clyde Quimby, Emboyd Theatre operator, dies
February 1940	First regional showing of *Gone With The Wind* at Emboyd Theatre
June 1952	Alliance Amusement Company leases Emboyd Theatre and name changes to Embassy Theatre
1968	Fox Realty Company sells building to Alliance Amusement Company
1970	Alliance Amusement Company sells building to Cinecom Corporation
1971	Indiana Hotel closes
1972	Cinecom Corporation declares bankruptcy and Embassy Theatre closes
Late 1972	Embassy Theatre Foundation is incorporated
March 1974	Bankruptcy court awards Embassy property to Solarsystems, Inc.
Spring 1974	Embassy Theatre Foundation begins to present shows in theatre; Sportservice Company acquires Embassy property from Solarsystems, Inc.
August 1974	Embassy Theatre Foundation signs agreement with Sportservice Company to purchase building
June 1975	Embassy Theatre Foundation acquires building
November 1985	First Festival of Trees takes place
1995	Major renovation enlarges theatre stage and orchestra pit and restores hotel lobby and mezzanine
2003	Walkway of Fame sidewalk installation marks Embassy Theatre's seventy-fifth anniversary
2005	State-of-the-art marquee and vertical sign installed
2008	Embassy celebrates eightieth anniversary

Emilie Boyd Quimby.
Embassy Theatre Foundation archives

W. Clyde Quimby.
Embassy Theatre Foundation archives

INTRODUCTION

The Embassy Theatre, Indiana's largest historic theatre, opened its doors May 14, 1928. It was originally named the Emboyd Theatre as a tribute to Emilie "Em" Boyd Quimby. She was the mother of W. Clyde Quimby, the first lessee/manager of the theatre. The name was changed to the Embassy in 1952 when the Alliance Theatre chain purchased the Emboyd.

From its beginning, the Embassy impacted the entertainment scene in Fort Wayne and northeastern Indiana. With more than three thousand seats, it was by far the largest and grandest of the city's theatres, bringing in the nation's top entertainers as well as first-run movies. In the mid-1960s, however, it began to lose its position as an entertainment venue and eventually closed.

In the early 1970s, when the building was threatened with demolition, a small group of individuals formed the Embassy Theatre Foundation, Inc., a nonprofit organization with the goal of saving the theatre complex and operating it as a performing arts theatre for the community. In the thirty-five years since that time, many improvements have been made, including new heating and cooling equipment, a state-of-the-art expanded stage, and improved seating.

Today, the Embassy is again a premier showplace. It hosts the Fort Wayne Philharmonic, Broadway touring companies, top entertainers, organ performances, various music concerts, speakers, comedians, youth, and various local-area performers.

This book is a brief history and description of the historic building that houses both the Embassy Theatre and the Indiana Hotel. It has been written to commemorate the theatre's 80th anniversary.

EMBASSY

ESTABLISHED 1928

THE THEATRE

THE HISTORIC FORT WAYNE
EMBASSY THEATRE

At the northwest corner of the building, the intersection of Jefferson Boulevard and Harrison Street, the Embassy features large, shallow windows that once displayed store wares. *Photo by Steve Linsenmayer*

THE THEATRE

One of the most important buildings constructed in the 1920s during Fort Wayne, Indiana's great building boom housed the Emboyd (now the Embassy) Theatre and the Indiana Hotel. The imposing structure occupied a quarter block on the southeast corner of Jefferson Boulevard and Harrison Street at the site of the former Plymouth Congregational Church. Today, the building's large scale and period architecture remain notable and impressive features of the downtown landscape.

In the 1920s the movie business was a lucrative focus for the entertainment industry. W. Clyde Quimby, whose organization managed four of Fort Wayne's most popular theatres, the Palace, Jefferson, Allen, and Strand, recognized the need for a newer and larger theatre to accommodate the growing popularity of movies. City business leaders agreed with Mr. Quimby that the city could support a new and larger movie house to participate in this popular pastime, and consequently the Fox Realty Company began construction of the Emboyd in 1926. Charles M. Niezer, president of the First National Bank, along with members of his wife's family, Oscar and Robert Fox, provided the $1,500,000 capital for the project. The primary architect was Alvin M. Strauss, a well-known local professional who designed other theatres throughout the Midwest as well as notable buildings in Fort Wayne such as the Grand Leader Department Store and the Sheridan Apartment Building. He and Edmond L. Miller, chief draftsman and designer for Strauss, brought in John Eberson, a nationally recognized architect for many of the nation's largest and best-known theatres. Eberson served as consultant and contributed to the interior design. The primary contractor was the local firm of Max Irmscher and Sons.

Above. Although the statue in the arch on the right was not included in final construction, this portion of the theatre's original blueprints provides a detailed view of the theatre auditorium side wall. *Embassy Theatre Foundation archives*

Below. Steel beams form the supports for the hotel during construction in 1927. *Embassy Theatre Foundation archives*

On opening night, May 14, 1928, the Emboyd blade sign set the night sky ablaze. *Embassy Theatre Foundation archives*

From the very beginning, the Emboyd created a strong impression on the community, beginning with its colorful, brightly lit, and oversized marquee. The Emboyd sign was the largest vertical sign in the state. It extended more than five stories above the marquee and weighed more than five tons. Each letter was 3½ feet tall. Using 3,500 incandescent light bulbs that required 31,000 watts of electrical power, the sign illuminated the entire block of Jefferson Boulevard.

Originally, the box office was in the center of the entrance to the theatre with doors on either side. Over the years, its location changed several times. Today it occupies an interior space to the west of the theatre (approximately where the hotel dining room used to be).

Entering the theatre, patrons pass through a vestibule with a modified Spanish design. Benou jaune, a rare French marble, covers the sidewalls. The highly decorative ceiling features an intricate geometric design. With the exception of two doors on either side of the vestibule (one allowing access from the Grand Wayne Convention Center sky bridge, which opened in January 1985, and the other entry from the box office area), the vestibule remains today essentially as it was in 1928. Wall plaques recognize individuals who founded the Embassy Theatre Foundation in the early 1970s.

Beyond the vestibule the outer lobby reflects an Italian architectural influence and features a number of small crystal chandeliers. Embedded in the black-and-white marble floor is a compass-like star, studded with a tiny triangle that points directly toward the magnetic North Pole. Wall plaques listing volunteers who have made significant contributions to the theatre through the past thirty-five years hang on the east wall.

Facing page. In their rush to enter the theatre, patrons often miss one of the most stunning features of the Embassy, the vestibule ceiling. *Photo by Steve Vorderman*

Above. The outer lobby in 1929, called "the black and white" by Embassy staff because of its checkerboard marble floor, featured the theatre call board, at far left, and posts embedded in the marble floor. The original chandeliers still hang in the lobby. *Embassy Theatre Foundation archives*

Between the outer lobby and the grand lobby is the original callboard. Ushers, stationed at various aisles throughout the auditorium, would signal the location of vacant seats in their area to the house captain by pressing call buttons located throughout the theatre. The house captain then directed latecomers to available seating. The system is still operable, although no longer used, and the brass callboard with its many signal lights still hangs on the west wall.

The grand lobby is an impressive space where patrons gather before performances and during intermissions. A thirty-six-foot-high barrel ceiling—lavishly decorated and painted in crimson, azure, and ivory—covers the one-hundred-foot-long room. Two crystal chandeliers and original ornate wall lamps illuminate the space. The tiled lobby floor is hand-laid in lavagno marble. Patrons will notice the floor tile has breaks in the pattern. Artisans who installed the floor would occasionally break the tile mold as a signature of their individual work. Five entrances off the lobby lead into the main floor of the auditorium.

In 1928, the grand lobby featured heavy burgundy-and-gold draperies that hung from every arch and alcove. *Embassy Theatre Foundation archives*

The decorative plaster on the lobby walls is unique. It features a variety of objects, including lions, jesters, gargoyles, flowers, and birds. Artisans first drew these objects to full scale. Next, an ornamental modeler created molds for each one. Finally, craftsmen transferred thousands of plaster castings, still wet, to a mesh laid in the walls. When dry, the puzzle was complete. The intricate plaster walls are lovingly maintained and appear much as they did in 1928.

A staircase at the far south end of the lobby leads to the lower lounges. Steps, which include intricate tile patterns on the risers, eventually open into a long hallway under the grand lobby floor. Pillared arches in a Spanish motif with carvings of the scarab beetle (*Scarabaeus sacer,* regarded by the ancient Egyptians as sacred and a symbol for new life), run the entire length of the hall. False back-lighted windows on one side of the corridor give an open-air impression even though the hall is below ground level. Off the hallway, tiled walls and a grand fireplace (although never operable) are features of the men's smoking lounge. The elegant and recently remodeled ladies lounge nearby includes carpeting and retains the original green, stenciled wall tiles. In 2006, the ladies lounge was expanded to more than twice the original size. Several foundations and women's groups contributed to this renovation, which greatly reduces waiting lines for entry into the lounge.

Right. This plaster jester overlooks the theatre lobby. *Photo by Steve Vorderman*

Below. At the far end of the lower-level corridor is an ornately designed men's smoking lounge. *Embassy Theatre Foundation archives*

Mounted along the walls are outlet openings for the central vacuum system, a total of 112 located throughout the building. Although the mechanism is no longer used, the Emboyd was one of the first public facilities with a central vacuum system.

Back on the main floor the broad staircase with partially carpeted marble steps and a majestic twenty-foot mirror leads from the grand lobby up to the mezzanine. There is another marble staircase to the mezzanine off the outer lobby. For many years, draperies framed the mirrors as well as the archways and coves along the grand staircase and the mezzanine. Today, many wedding ceremonies are performed on the landing of the staircase.

The mezzanine runs the length of the lobby. Installed in 1985, its custom-woven carpeting features the same medallion motif installed throughout the theatre in 1928.

The music room at the north end of the mezzanine overlooks the grand lobby and is an intimate gathering place for patrons. Originally, the room housed private parties and

The grand staircase serves as the focal point of the theatre lobby.
Photo by Steve Vorderman

Above. Artistic details were carefully integrated into all pieces of the building, from moldings and carpet to balustrades and columns.
Photo by Steve Vorderman

Below. The mezzanine, or second floor, of the theatre overlooks the grand lobby to the left and gives access to loge and upper balcony seats to the right. *Embassy Theatre Foundation archives*

The oldest photograph of the auditorium was taken before the 1928 opening night and captures the footlights, no longer a part of the stage, at bottom. *Embassy Theatre Foundation archives*

receptions before and after concerts. As needs of the theatre changed over the years, the area was used for a variety of purposes, including as a wine bar and even as office space. Recently, it has been returned to its original purpose.

A Packard piano built for the Emboyd by the Packard Piano Company of Fort Wayne once stood in the music room. Today a large grand piano, once belonging to Robert Goldstine, stands there. Goldstine was a long-time, generous supporter of the theatre and first president of the Embassy Theatre Foundation. At his death in 2001, the piano was purchased from his estate and donated to the Embassy by Mark Suedhoff. Today pianists again welcome theatre patrons with music.

The sheer size of the auditorium makes a lasting impression on patrons entering the balcony from the mezzanine. The room is 110 feet wide by 140 feet in length. The main dome is 80 feet above the main floor. The balcony sweeps up the east wall of the building and extends over the lobby ceiling below. A steel girder (11 feet high, 110 feet long, and weighing 200 tons) supports the balcony, which seats 1,070 people. The girder was designed with a plus-four factor, meaning the balcony can safely accommodate the weight of four persons to each seat.

Suspended above the uppermost balcony seats, the projection booth houses two 35mm film projectors, spot lights, and the original Brenograph projector, a portion of which is visible at lower right. *Photo by Steve Linsenmayer*

The ceiling of the auditorium features a large decorative oval which is lighted by the theatre's three-color lighting system. It matches the lighting system in the balcony-side wall coves and the lighting surrounding the proscenium. The large oval acts as a sound baffle to the balcony, projecting sound from the stage down to the balcony. Many patrons feel that, although they are further from the stage performers, they hear a more intimate sound in the balcony than elsewhere in the auditorium.

At the top of the balcony is a door leading to a stairway to the projection booth. The stairway is suspended outside the east wall of the building. Because motion picture film was highly flammable in the 1920s, the location and construction of both the projection booth and the stairway prevented any potential fires from spreading into the auditorium. The stairway is now enclosed and protected from the elements.

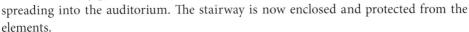

The projection booth contains two massive 35mm film projectors, a 16mm projector, several Xenon traveling spotlights, and a variety of sound equipment, amplifiers, and controls. The projectors were updated to reflect current industry standards and can show any film speed, a plus for showing old silent movies. In addition, there is a rare Brenograph, the only original 1928 piece of equipment remaining in the booth. The machine can project sing-a-long words and other special effects onto the auditorium screen. Because it uses carbon rods for illumination, it is seldom used today since replacement rods are difficult to obtain.

In the projection booth is a trap door that leads to the area above the auditorium ceiling. In the space between the ceiling and actual roof are catwalks which allow access to lights surrounding the interior ceiling dome. Catwalks also lead to the ceiling spotlights that focus primarily on the stage. As they travel the catwalks adjusting the high intensity spotlights, stagehands can catch glimpses of the auditorium seats eighty feet below through the many small openings in the ceiling.

When built, the auditorium boasted almost 3,100 seats with the main floor of the auditorium containing more than 1,900 seats, arranged in a semi-circle on a sloping floor that allowed maximum sight lines to the stage. However, a number of seats were removed to provide seating for those with disabilities as well as space to enlarge the stage. Total seating capacity today, including the balcony, is 2,471. Seat bottoms range from 15.5 inches wide to 18.8 inches wide, due to the curve of the rows. The majority of seats are 16.5 inches wide. Fastened to a number of seatbacks are brass plates engraved with the names of various contributors to the Embassy Theatre Foundation.

Along the walls of the auditorium are sculptured relief patterns of birds, flowers, coats-of-arms, and figures depicting music, comedy, and tragedy. The valances draping the side walls are the only original 1928 drapery material remaining in the building. The light coves under the balcony and on the side walls of the balcony each have three color circuits (red, white, and blue). Stagehands control them from the lightboard located backstage and can achieve a variety of hues with the intricate dimming system. There are more than four thousand individual lightbulbs in the theatre. In 2007 a new state-of-the-art lightboard and dimmer system were installed. The computerized control desk can be operated by one individual and is movable to any location on the stage floor as well as the rear of the auditorium. The original 1928 lightboard was fifteen feet long and ten feet high and required two to three operators. Today, a single operator sits in the back row of the main floor and can, with the flick of a finger, control all house and stage lighting.

Two large chandeliers hang on either side of the proscenium arch. The chandeliers, along with lights in the main dome, are the principle sources of auditorium lighting. Each of the eight-foot chandeliers weighs five hundred pounds, holds 64 lightbulbs, and uses two thousand watts of electricity. Draperies behind the chandeliers hide the openings of the organ chambers—large rooms that contain more than 1,300 pipes for the Grande Page pipe organ.

The Emboyd was the first air-cooled public building in Fort Wayne. A well, drilled beneath the floor of the second sub-level under the Harrison Street sidewalk, provided cool water that was pumped through a series of large pipes. Air from the auditorium circulated through and around the pipes. Cooled air returning to the auditorium was about 55 degrees. When built, the system was large enough to cool the equivalent of twelve thousand home refrigerators.

Coal furnaces originally heated the building. The alley on the south side of the building contained a number of openings for coal. Chutes descended almost three stories below ground level and emptied in front of six large coal furnaces below the auditorium. Today most of the original equipment is gone, although the system still uses the original 1928 blower. New gas furnaces and air conditioning equipment were installed in 1985. They heat and cool the building more efficiently and comfortably than was possible in 1928.

When built, the stage was approximately 80 feet wide, including wing space on each side. The proscenium arch, which frames the stage, was 55 feet across and 30 feet high. Working depth from the back wall to the lip of the stage was 26 feet. The gridiron or fly space—a large steel framework six stories above the stage floor—contained various curtains and stage rigging. Originally, there were 46 different lines that could lift (or fly) various sets or curtains. The pulley system was so perfectly counterweighted that one individual could easily hoist a set design weighing hundreds of pounds.

In 1928 and for years thereafter, the stage space was more than adequate to accommodate vaudeville acts and stage shows. As stage productions grew more elaborate, however, the stage fell short of minimum requirements. Improvements in the mid-1980s helped somewhat. Included were a new lambrequin (the drapery and swags topping the main stage curtain), new gridiron rigging, and a new computerized lighting system.

Still, improvements did not address the main difficulty of a stage that was too small to handle large touring companies. In late 1994, the board of directors with then-executive director, Doris Stovall, began a complete stage renovation. It was a $5 million project

Above. Emboyd operator W. Clyde Quimby stands in front of the original lightboard in 1928, with stage rigging to the right. *Embassy Theatre Foundation archives*

Overleaf. Few audience members get to see behind the stage curtains, which, at stage left, hide the rigging used to hang lights, drapes, and stage equipment. *Photo by Steve Vorderman*

covering two years. The first phase involved removal of the backstage wall along with all the Hotel Indiana rooms facing Harrison Street. The resulting seven-story space permitted construction of a new stage wall and provided an additional twenty-five feet of stage depth. Today there is no discernable difference to the Harrison Street façade. The back of the stage wall, however, is now only a few feet from the windows. Enlarging the stage apron, another of the renovation projects, allowed for more space on the orchestra lift, which can handily accommodate up to fifty-five musicians and can be moved up to stage level or lowered down into the pit, out of sight. When at stage level it provides even more stage floor space.

Increased by more than 40 feet in renovation to a depth of 67 feet, the Embassy now rivals the finest stages in the country. The blonde maple stage flooring is sprung for dance and can withstand up to 150 pounds per square inch. There are now 58 lines rigged to fly various stage sets, an increase of 12 lines. These improvements provide ample space for

the orchestra shell used most often by the Fort Wayne Philharmonic, elaborate staging needed for large touring companies, and programs that require a large musical group in the pit.

The improvements made to the stage also more perfectly match the acoustically correct auditorium. The excellent sound disbursement, inherent in the design of the building, along with direct sight lines to the stage, are obvious from every seat of the auditorium.

Below the stage are ten dressing rooms: one star dressing room, seven principal dressing rooms, and two chorus dressing rooms. Each is fitted with a lavatory and lighted mirrors. The star dressing room contains a sitting area along with a private bath. The area also contains storage rooms, a laundry room, and the traditional green room, which today serves as the business office for show road managers and promoters.

Over the years, artisans from various touring groups painted elaborate scenes depicting their productions on corridor walls leading to the dressing rooms. Although worthy and artistic, the murals could not be cleaned or painted. Consequently, it was decided to take pictures of the wall art and hang the large photographs in the same spaces where they were first painted. Today, the clean, painted corridors contain a pictorial history of the shows and performances that appeared at the Embassy during the 1980s.

Dressing room no. 1, the star's dressing room, features a sitting area and a private bathroom. The room is personalized, per a detailed contract rider, to each performer's needs and requests. *Photo by Steve Linsenmayer*

Logos and actors' signatures from shows such as *South Pacific,*
An Evening with Burt Reynolds, and *Tap Dance Kid* were painted
on the backstage walls. *Embassy Theatre Foundation archives*

Early in the twentieth century, community leaders understood the cultural value and the economic sense of building a large and opulent theatre. When they expended considerable financial resources to build the Emboyd Theatre, they made a statement about the value of the performing arts to the Fort Wayne area. In return, the community has continued to invest in the theatre. Local foundations such as Foellinger, Community, English Bonter Mitchell, and Goldstine have taken the lead in supporting the theatre. Today, through the generosity of the region's corporate and private citizens, the Embassy Theatre is able to offer worldclass entertainment in a beautiful and efficient building that is truly a showplace of northeastern Indiana.

The console of the four manual/sixteen rank Grande
Page pipe organ today. *Photo by Steve Vorderman*

2

THE ORGAN

There are few sounds as thrilling as the rich and sonorous tones of the Embassy's Grande Page pipe organ spilling into the auditorium. And nothing in the moviegoer's experience is quite as dramatic as watching the organ console rise from the depths of the orchestra pit.

In the days of silent movies most theatres could not afford a full orchestra to accompany the film. Most movie houses chose to employ individual pit musicians, with the smaller houses using a piano. The larger ones, however, preferred a theatre pipe organ which emulated a full-sized orchestra. It was much more economical to employ one organist than to pay for a fully staffed orchestra. With an auditorium originally seating more than three thousand people, Embassy developers chose an organ appropriately scaled to the house. Both the design and installation of the instrument took advantage of the auditorium's excellent acoustic properties.

The Page Pipe Organ Company of Lima, Ohio, a manufacturer of small organs, built only four large instruments. One is unaccounted for. A second is in a theatre in Avalon on Santa Catalina off the California coast and a third is being installed in a high school near Atlanta, Georgia. That organ had previously served a Chicago radio station, WHT, owned by the Wrigley family. During construction of the Emboyd, developers installed the fourth large Page pipe organ at a cost of approximately $42,000. In today's currency that amount is the equivalent of hundreds of thousands of dollars. Thus, the Grande Page is rare and one of the few theatre pipe organs in the nation still located at its original site.

When it was built in 1928, the Grande Page console was reddish with gold accents; today it is white with gold filigree. *Embassy Theatre Foundation archives*

Theatre organs differ from typical church organs because they are designed to reproduce the sounds of a symphony orchestra in order to accompany silent movies. Consequently, theatre organs contain imitative stops such as a tuba, violin, saxophone, and clarinet and operate under much higher wind pressures than church organs. Further, theatre organs are highly unified in that almost any musically useful effect is obtainable from a limited number of ranks or sets of pipes. At installation the Emboyd pipe organ consisted of fifteen ranks of pipes controlled from a four-manual (keyboard) console. Pipes range in size from that of a small pencil to large wooden flues sixteen feet high. Chambers behind the large chandeliers on each side of the theatre's proscenium, which is the arch that frames the stage, hold the approximately thirteen hundred pipes. The chambers also contain a number of other instruments including a glockenspiel, xylophone, marimba, piano, drums, cymbals, and castanets. There are also a number of special effects such as a fire gong, police siren, bird whistles, telephone bell, automobile horn, and train whistle. These all allow the organists to match their accompaniment to the actions of silent movies.

Left. The organ chambers house a wide variety of pipes, such as reeds, in the foreground, brass trumpets, center, and wooden flute pipes, back. *Embassy Theatre Foundation archives*

Below. Percussive instruments are located in the main organ chamber, including a hand-painted drum, at left. *Embassy Theatre Foundation archives*

There were many house organists through the years. Percy Robbins was the first. Trained in the classics, Robbins had been associated with the Balaban and Katz Theater circuit in Chicago. The talk of the town, he was a dapper gentleman who dressed in impeccably tailored suits, wore an ascot, and carried an elaborate walking stick. Marguerite Hitzeman was another house organist. A local musician, she had earlier been studio organist for radio station WOWO. At one time, famed celebrity Marilyn (Marvel) Maxwell's mother sat in as assistant organist. And Jean Brown Bosselmann, another local personality, used to broadcast organ programs from the theatre.

Buddy Nolan was the best known of all the organists. In the late 1940s, Nolan visited Fort Wayne to see an old army friend. When he learned there was an organ in the Emboyd Theatre, he asked to play it and fell in love immediately. Taken with the rich sounds of the Page pipe organ, he moved to Fort Wayne and started playing electronic organs in various local restaurants—just to be near the object of his affection.

In 1952, the Alliance Theatre chain assumed operation of the Emboyd, changed the name to Embassy, and hired Nolan as house organist. Before every showing of a featured picture (several times a day, six days a week), Nolan played the organ, a commitment that often required that he speed across town in his small European sports car from whichever restaurant he was playing in, so that he could get to the theatre on time.

Eventually, the organ interludes became almost as popular as the film features. The Alliance management was supportive and provided funding for special effects. Extensive costuming, special lighting including black light, sing-a-longs, and special graphics projected on the movie screen enhanced the organ pieces.

In the late 1950s the demanding performance schedule in Fort Wayne and the lure of California drew Nolan to the West Coast clubs. He often visited Avalon on Santa Catalina Island to play the Page organ located there. He also returned periodically to Fort Wayne just to play the Grande Page at the Embassy.

By 1960 the organ had fallen into disrepair and needed attention. Bob Ort, a longtime friend of Nolan's, invited Bob Nickerson, a local organ fan, technician, and engineer, to meet and talk with Buddy about repairing the organ. With little money but a lot of advice from organ builder Al Buzby, Nickerson, under Buddy's direction, made the necessary repairs and, by late 1961, the Grande Page was again ready to be heard and enjoyed.

In 1962 Nolan moved back to Indiana and resumed his duties as Embassy house organist. Shortly after his return, he instituted a series called *Theatre Organ at Midnight*. These programs began at midnight because the movie schedule ran to 11 PM. Even at that late hour, large audiences of locals as well as organ enthusiasts from Ohio, Illinois, and Michigan attended. Once, a large number of fans from Detroit chartered a private railroad car hooked up to the Wabash Cannonball passenger train, and rode to Fort Wayne—just to attend a midnight concert.

The shows were more than organ recitals. They featured special effects, including stage decorations, guest vocalists, calliopes, audience hecklers, and even a lighted crystal ball.

Facing page, top. Young Buddy Nolan stands at the Grande Page console in the late 1940s. *Embassy Theatre Foundation archives*

Facing page, bottom. This drawing was used by Buddy Nolan as his promotional calling card and was signed by Nolan at bottom right in 1962. *Embassy Theatre Foundation archives*

To Bud Berges
One of the very best!
Buddy Nolan
3-21-62

A regular part of all but the first two midnight concerts featured Dyne Pfeffenberger at a white grand piano which rose from the orchestra pit with Nolan and he playing piano and organ duets.

In all, there were ten *Theatre Organ at Midnight* concerts. As a fundraising event for the Embassy Theatre Foundation, Nolan's final performance attracted more than two thousand people. Over the course of his years as the house organist, Nolan made two record albums: *Theatre Organ at Midnight* and *After Midnight*. Both are no longer available except as collector's items.

By the early 1970s, the management of the theatre had changed hands again and the building began to show signs of neglect. Eventually, the theatre closed and the management firm filed for bankruptcy. There was talk of converting the hotel to a senior housing complex and razing the theatre for a parking lot.

During this time a small group of organ devotees, including Buddy Nolan, began gathering at the theatre on Saturday mornings. With permission to maintain the organ, they repaired small air leaks, tuned pipes, and tried to keep it in playing condition. Through their efforts, the organ survived the dark days before the foundation acquired the building in 1975. Instrumental in this group were Byron Fogt, Robert Nickerson, Ellsworth Smith, and Bill Zabel.

The newly formed Embassy Theatre Foundation realized the organ was a focal point of theatre operations and that there was strong community support to preserve it. Other

This is the last publicity photograph of Buddy Nolan at the Grande Page. *Embassy Theatre Foundation archives*

Patrons crowd the theatre lobby during intermission of a *Theatre Organ at Midnight* concert in the 1963–64 season. *Embassy Theatre Foundation archives*

needs, however, took precedence. The building needed a new heating plant. The roof leaked. The organ therefore had to wait its turn.

With the eventual completion of the building's most crucial repairs, the foundation turned its attention to the organ in the mid-1980s. The Saturday-morning group had kept the organ playable through the decade with ingenious use of adhesive tape, paper clips, and elbow grease. Despite these efforts, the organ keyboards and pedal board were badly worn, the pneumatic system worked erratically, and the wind chests that held the pipes were warped and leaked air. Even the original note relay system had failed and was replaced by an electronic system designed and built by Bill Zabel, one of the Saturday morning technicians. The instrument was showing signs of its sixty years of use.

Buddy Nolan passed away in April 1986. He was active in Embassy Theatre activities almost to the date of his death. As a tribute to his dedication to the preservation of the theatre organ, the American Theatre Organ Society (ATOS) named Nolan to its Hall of Fame in 1977. This same organization named Robert Goldstine to its Hall of Fame in 2001, an appropriate and justified accolade for two of the Embassy Theatre's staunchest supporters.

Shortly after Nolan's death, the Fort Wayne Woman's Club, as a memorial to Buddy, organized a number of fundraisers for a trust fund to benefit the organ. Also, the Wilson Foundation contributed funds for the organ project. Most importantly, the Embassadors—a group of Embassy volunteers—contributed a large portion of the proceeds from their annual Festival of Trees to the organ restoration fund. The foundation finally had funds to begin major restoration.

Chaired by Byron Fogt, the organ committee had two major goals: to add a rank of reed pipes to the main chamber and to expand and improve the electronic relay system.

Members chose to add the additional rank of pipes themselves and purchased a brass trumpet rank from the Trivo Company in Hagerstown, Maryland. They installed the rank of pipes in the left, or main, chamber. The right, or solo, chamber contained two ranks that spoke at a high volume: the English post horn and the kinura. With the addition of the brass trumpet to the main chamber, the balance between the two chambers greatly improved. Incorporation of the new rank has been the only tonal modification of the organ since it was installed in 1928.

Because improvements to the console and electronic systems requires special knowledge, the committee contracted Carlton B. Smith of then J. K. Aikman Company of Indianapolis. Smith, a recognized restorer and Page organ specialist, received the console at the Indianapolis shop in May 1988. In addition to repairing and redecorating the console itself, he also installed a new Peterson electromagnetic stop action, a Trousdale eight-memory combination action, a new pedal board with additional toe studs, and added the capability of recording the organ through a backstage computer. All of these improvements greatly enhanced the reliability and functionality of the organ and increased the response speed to the organist's registration changes.

With the console out for repairs, the committee decided to adjust and rebuild some of the percussion instruments, including the chrysoglott, an instrument of metal bars struck by felt hammers. It also performed extensive re-leathering and re-wiring work to the wooden wind chests that held the organ pipes. In addition, it procured a Page wind chest and placed it in the main chamber to accommodate the new trumpet rank.

Left. Byron Fogt, the foundation's organ crew chief for nearly thirty years, tunes a brass reed pipe by adjusting the length of the tuning wire. Each organ pipe must be individually tuned. *Photo by Ray Soughan; Embassy Theatre Foundation archives*

Below. Byron Fogt and John Foell, current organ crew chief, display pipes removed from the organ chest. *Embassy Theatre Foundation archives*

North American Van Lines donated the truck used to transport the Grande Page console to Indianapolis for repairs in summer 1988. *Embassy Theatre Foundation archives*

Smith completed the console renovation in September 1988. In better shape than ever, the organ was ready once again to resume its original task—accompanying silent films. The first public concert of the renewed Page featured Chicago organist Jeff Weiler accompanying the silent film classic *Phantom of the Opera*. It was a Halloween performance.

Both nationally and internationally recognized artists have given concerts on the Grande Page. They include Barry Baker, Don Baker, Gaylord Carter, Dennis James, Lyn Larsen, and Walt Strony. Also included are Ken Double, Simon Gledhill, Tom Hazelton, John Muri, Ron Rhode, Jim Riggs, Clark Wilson, and Fort Wayne native Mark Herman. Many others have played organ programs or accompanied films at the Embassy, and all who do so marvel at the majestic and responsive sound of the Page organ. The organ is still lovingly maintained by a group of dedicated volunteers currently headed by John Foell. The group ranges from seasoned engineers and technicians to teenagers who are discovering the magic of theatre organs.

The American Theatre Organ Society has convened five national meetings in Indianapolis. At each, hundreds of participants have traveled as a group to Fort Wayne to hear top organists play the Grande Page pipe organ. To demonstrate its esteem for the instrument, the society placed the Embassy Theatre and its pipe organ on the National Registry of Historic and Significant Instruments. The Grande Page pipe organ remains the voice and the soul of the theatre today.

Hundreds of stop tabs encircle the four manuals, or keyboards, of the Grande Page console. *Photo by Steve Vorderman*

Theatre Organ

JOURNAL OF THE AMERICAN THEATRE ORGAN SOCIETY

Hitting the High Note

46 INDIANAPOLIS

46 INDIANAPOLIS

2001 – The 46th Annual Convention of the American Theatre Organ Society

ADMIT ONE - Good Date Only

http://www.atos.org

March / April 2001

The Grande Page has graced three covers of the American Theatre Organ Society's international magazine. *Embassy Theatre Foundation archives*

It was for the joy of playing the Grande Page that community leaders such as Bob Goldstine worked tirelessly and passionately to save the Embassy building. *Photo courtesy of Dyne Pfeffenberger*

Only two of the original 1928 Emboyd usher staff are identified in this photo: usher captain Hoy McConnel, front, and Charlie Dailey, top row, far left. *Embassy Theatre Foundation archives*

3

THE PERFORMERS

The Emboyd Theatre celebrated its grand opening on May 14, 1928, with the rollicking silent film *Easy Come, Easy Go.* Also on the bill was the *Honorable Mr. Wu and His Chinese Nights Revue,* a song and dance act; Charles Bennington with his Harmonica Band; Frank Richardson (the Joy Boy of Song); Percy Robbins playing the Grande Page pipe organ; and the theatre orchestra playing under the baton of Wilbur Pickett. Cost of attending this extravaganza was 60 cents.

Over the years, thousands of performers have hit the Embassy boards to entertain Fort Wayne. Highlights of each decade follow.

THE 1920S

Bob Hope appeared at the theatre for the first time in 1928 and again in 1938. Although unsubstantiated, old-timers say Hope spoke the first lines of his show business career on the Emboyd stage.

THE 1930S

Nobellette and Ryan, a comedy team, gave a live stage performance which included Irene Ryan, who later gained fame as Granny in the popular television show *Beverly Hillbillies.* Other performers in 1931 included the Mills Brothers ("a swell bunch of guys," according to Bud Berger, stage manager of the Emboyd) and several appearances by the comedy team Amos and Andy.

This advertisement for the Emboyd's opening night was placed in the
May 12, 1928, edition of the Fort Wayne *News-Sentinel. Embassy Theatre
Foundation archives; used with permission of the Fort Wayne* News-Sentinel

Dec. 25
1938

To my Pal Bud Berg
Thanks for The Memory
Bob Hope

Maurice Seymour
CHICAGO

Bob Hope was among the first of many famous people to perform
at the Embassy. *Embassy Theatre Foundation archives*

In 1931 when gangster films such as *The Public Enemy* and *Little Caesar* were popular,
a young gunman held up the Emboyd box office staff. According to newspaper reports,

> . . . at 10:45 o'clock Sunday night a gunman ransacked the safe in the office, taking $1,880
> in cash. He made his escape with an accomplice who waited for him outside the theater in
> a speedy sedan.

The Emboyd house orchestra in 1931–32 identified, from left, as
L. Stuckey, F. Senneider, H. Baier, K. Conner, director Ted Conner,
Duke Baier, R. Wharten, A. Willis, W. "Bip" Sawyer, and Dick Richard.
Embassy Theatre Foundation archives

In 1932 Fort Wayne natives Ole Olsen and Chic Johnson opened an original vaudeville revue called *Soup to Nuts.* An instant success, New York City backers changed the name to *Hellzapoppin* and put it on the national circuit. According to Betty Stein, local newspaper columnist, one of the funniest memories of the show was a man running down the aisle with a small potted tree calling for "Mrs. Smith." He did this several times and each time the tree was bigger and taller. At the end of the show he was up in the tree in the lobby! It brought down the house.

In March 1933, the Emboyd featured *The George White Scandals,* a major road show billed as America's Greatest Musical Revue. The production featured tap dancer Eleanor Powell, a top MGM star, as well as the famous Broadway Beauties and the comedy team of Willie and Eugene Howard. Patrons paid 40 cents for a matinee and 55 cents for the evening show. Nineteen thirty-three also saw the appearance of Nick Lucas who gained fame by introducing the song *Singin' in the Rain.*

In December 1933, the midnight production of *Strike Me Pink* ran for five days and provided work for twelve stagehands. The company included James Barton, Leota Lane, and Connie Cromwell. Real stars of the show, however, were two fellows named Frank Fay and Jack Lenny. Fay later originated the role of Elwood Dowd on Broadway in the show *Harvey.* According to notes of Bud Berger, the company drank three cases of beer a day. On the last day, they drank the new 6 percent beer.

Early in the year 1935, Clyde Quimby, well-known Emboyd Theatre operator and showman, died. Among the stars who appeared at the Emboyd in 1935 was comedian Fred Allen, who emceed a show called *Town Hall Tonight.*

In November of that year the O'Connor Family appeared. Described as a show with "a little bit of everything," it included a 5-year-old girl named Pat and her 10-year-old

Stage manager Bud Berger collected autographed publicity photos and often wrote details, such as the names of each O'Connor family member, including Don at center left, directly on the photos in fountain pen. *Embassy Theatre Foundation archives*

cousin, Donald, who later appeared in many major movie musicals. Pat's mother, Nellie, was the main dancer in the act. Bud Berger reported that she tore her fur coat and the wives of the Fort Wayne stagehands mended it.

The Great Depression impacted everyone by 1936. As an enticement to come to the movies, the Emboyd sponsored its first Bank Night in May of that year. Patrons of the theatre entered their names in a register kept by the theatre. Names were drawn and, if the patron was in the theatre at that time, a cash prize of $100 was awarded.

In 1937, Harvey G. Cocks Sr. became general manager of the Quimby organization. Cocks brought with him broad theatrical experience. He also was a man with a social conscience who looked for opportunities to entertain underprivileged children. *Snow White and the Seven Dwarfs,* one of many first-run films shown at the theatre, broke all Emboyd box office records because Cocks gave free admission to six thousand underprivileged children.

In September 1938, about three thousand children saw *Boys Town* with Spencer Tracy and Mickey Rooney for free. In November, the Emboyd sponsored a Food Day. Every youth up to 15 years of age who brought a can of food to the theatre got free admission.

One of the benefit shows, dedicated to the memory of Clyde Quimby, starred Hal Kemp and his orchestra. Also appearing were songstress Judy Starr, Paul Ramos and His Wonder Midgets, romantic song stylist Bob Allan, Woo-Woo Man Jack LaMaire, and Mary Berghoff, Fort Wayne's own songbird. The film *Hard to Get,* starring Dick Powell and Olivia DeHavilland, ended the evening. Ticket prices were $1.50 and $2.

Going to a movie at the Emboyd was a magical experience. Uniformed ushers wearing white gloves and carrying a flashlight led moviegoers to their seats. Illuminated with a spotlight, the Grande Page organ rose from the depths of the orchestra pit, and music filled the auditorium. The organist played a fanfare, the red-and-gold curtains opened, the spotlight faded, the organ descended into the depths again, and the movie began.

Ed Crismore from Wells County, Indiana, remembers seeing his first talking picture at the Emboyd. He was 9 years old. He had helped his father clean chicken houses that day. They went directly to the theatre without changing clothes. Ed remembers that the usher seated them in a far corner.

Wizard of Oz opened in September 1939. It provided an escape for Fort Wayne audiences who worried over news of the German invasion of Poland and the start of World War II. As part of the publicity campaign for the movie, the *Journal Gazette,* one of Fort Wayne's daily newspapers, sponsored a contest and offered prizes of $3, $2, a copy of the novel, and free movie tickets.

Mr. Smith Goes to Washington, however, was the Emboyd's surprise top-grosser of 1939. It sold more tickets than *Wizard of Oz.*

THE 1940S

The first Fort Wayne showing of *Gone with the Wind* dazzled audiences in February 1940. The movie ran for a week with three showings daily. Crowds lined Jefferson and Harrison streets for each screening. Ed Crismore skipped his high school classes, hopped on the 7 AM interurban train in Kingsland, Indiana, and made his way to the theatre. Returning to school the next day, his punishment was to present a review of the movie for his speech class.

Fort Wayne welcomed Marilyn (Marvel) Maxwell back to her hometown in May 1940. She was a vocalist at the time with the Ted Weems Orchestra. A young man named Perry Como also was singing with the Weems group. They did four shows a day. Marilyn went on to star in Hollywood pictures at MGM. A favorite of Bob Hope, she performed with him on radio, in movies, and on his G.I. tours.

Herbie Kay and his orchestra also performed in May with three shows a day. Jackie Leonard was the featured comedian with Kay. Orchestra leader Bob Crosby and his Bobcats did four shows a day in June 1940. It was a very successful run—partly due to a cute blonde singer named Doris Day, who was a member of the group.

Perry Como. *Embassy Theatre Foundation archives*

The *George White Scandals* appeared again at the Emboyd in November and December of that year. The show featured comedy routines by Ben Blue and The Three Stooges. They appeared at the personal invitation of their old friend Harvey Cocks Sr.

During World War II, the theatre was primarily a movie house. In 1942, Paramount Pictures produced *Star Spangled Rhythm,* an all-star hit that proved to be the Emboyd's biggest grosser of the year. That year also saw the first Victory War Booth in Fort Wayne.

It stood in the lobby of the theatre. Lon Chaney Jr. and actress Elyse Knox were in town for the first War Bond Drive. In 1944 the theatre managers received the following message:

> Following are your instructions for "V-Day." If Peace is declared prior to our opening on "V-Day," all of our theaters will be closed. If after opening, cease ticket sales, complete film run, (then) spill house, and lock it up for the day. Naturally, you will make an announcement that Peace has been declared!

There were some issues with popcorn in the mid-1940s. The following memo from the management explains why popcorn sales temporarily stopped:

> Whoever is spreading popcorn on the sidewalk in front of the theater must discontinue this practice. We will soon have a marquee full of pigeons!

Some of the Emboyd's top grossing movies of the 1940s included Betty Grable in *Coney Island,* Alice Faye in *Hello Frisco, Hello,* Mickey Rooney and Judy Garland in *Girl Crazy,* and William Bendix in *Guadalcanal Diary.*

Many soldiers stationed in Fort Wayne went to the movies. The management felt obliged to issue this word of caution to the cashier:

> Talking to soldiers in front of the box office is not allowed—that is unnecessary conversation! Let's be patriotic about all of this!

Artie Shaw's orchestra was on stage in January 1945. The weather was foul with lots of snow and ice, but the show broke even financially. The big band era, however, was beginning to show signs of old age.

In 1947, radio station WGL broadcast the national radio program *Dr. IQ* from the Emboyd stage. With Lew Valentine as emcee, the program lasted six weeks and packed the theatre. At the first show, a patron won $1,000, which was a fortune in those days.

Artie Shaw.
*Embassy Theatre
Foundation archives*

NBC's Lew Valentine, at
right, was the star during
Radio WGL's stage pro-
duction of *Dr. IQ.*
*Reprinted with permission
of* The Journal Gazette,
Fort Wayne, Indiana

THE 1950S

Harvey Cocks Sr. left as general manager in 1951. The theatre at the time was taking strong measures to counteract the impact of television. Customers could exchange Fort Wayne transit tokens at the theatre box office, with the transit company covering the ticket costs. The staff added double features and equipped the theatre for Cinemascope, which showed movies on a much wider screen.

Although the management also tried to offer vaudeville shows, finding well-known stars to perform was a problem. In 1952, Frank Doyle, a trapeze artist, made an appearance, but stage manager Bud Berger said, "[I] had a hell of a time rigging it." The Six Tokayers (a teeter board act) shot a boy eighteen feet through the air into a chair. Berger reported that the group drove an old army bus that would only go thirty miles per hour. Hap Hazard and his partner, Mary Hart, performed a high wire act, did comedy, and played the accordion. Berger said they did a great job even though Hap forgot his lines.

Stage manager Bud Berger, at left, with stage hands
Al Brauer, George Waymaster, and Merle Wackerfellen.
Embassy Theatre Foundation archives

The Embassy concession stand in the early 1950s, shortly after Alliance Theatre purchased the building. *Embassy Theatre Foundation archives*

In June 1952, the Emboyd was sold to the Alliance Amusement Company. The new owner temporarily closed the theatre and redecorated. The company changed the name to the Embassy and reopened in October. Many teenagers of the 1950s remember Saturday night dates at the Embassy. Always dress-up occasions, the audience saw a newsreel, cartoon, previews of coming attractions, and the feature presentation. There was also an organ concert. A newspaper advertisement from 1953 advertised *The Girl Next Door,* a documentary on the coronation of Queen Elizabeth II and a concert at the Grande Page organ featuring Evelyn Osborne.

Bill Hughes and Blackie.
Embassy Theatre Foundation archives

Performances spotlighted hometown talent as well as big-name professionals. WOWO, a local radio station, sponsored *Stars of Tomorrow,* a talent show on the Embassy stage. Carolyn Yager, a teenager at the time, remembers the excitement of appearing on the stage. She sang *Blue Skies* with three of her classmates. Jack Underwood, WOWO announcer, was emcee that evening. Big-name performers who appeared on stage in the 1950s included standing-room-only performances by Fred Waring and his Singers as well as Fats Domino.

Fats Domino.
Embassy Theatre Foundation archives

THE 1960S

In 1963, Buddy Nolan gave a very successful midnight concert on the restored Grande Page pipe organ. It led to a series of *Theatre Organ at Midnight* concerts.

The death of Bud Berger in 1965 ended an important chapter in the Embassy history. Bud loved and understood show performers. He made them comfortable, met their needs, and listened to their tales of woe. Jack Benny and Bob Hope were among the many that sent their condolences.

Efforts to bring quality performances to the stage and screen continued into the 1970s. Phil Olofson, local promoter and Embassy board member, said, "We're interested in booking just about anything . . . concerts of all types, stage shows, travelogues, lectures and other attractions."

Hector Olivera, a young Argentinean organist, gave a brilliant concert to about twelve hundred patrons in December 1976. Journalist Sharon Little described one particular aspect of the show:

> A fascinating feature of the Christmas portion of the concert was a large tree decorated with lights, which responded, through some clever electrical hookup, to every musical mood of Olivera's organ. Brilliant sound, brilliantly lighted tree; delicate musical tone, same for the tree. A delightful sight-sound experience.

Several Broadway productions came to the Embassy in 1976. They included the musicals *Irene* and *Man of La Mancha*. The Bicentennial Celebration for 1976 included a concert featuring The United States Armed Forces Bicentennial Band and Chorus. In March there was a production of *Together Tonight,* a story of Jefferson, Hamilton, and Burr.

In 1977, after an appearance by a popular heavy metal group called Nazareth, the Embassy board banned hard rock concerts. A rowdy crowd had jammed the lobby that evening. There was a crash as an original light fixture fell off the wall. Although nobody established blame, the incident was enough to end, for a time, further appearances of hard rock groups.

The end of the decade brought a variety of outstanding performers. Comedians David Brenner and Victor Borge were solid hits. Red Skelton had two sell-out performances. At the conclusion of each show, Skelton graciously returned to the stage and talked informally with the audiences. A *Journal Gazette* reporter had this to say about the comedian:

> Laughter to Red Skelton must be like what rain is to the parched earth, refreshing and replenishing him with every guffaw, renewing his gentle spirit.
> Making the world laugh is no easy task. Having geniuses like Red Skelton around, however, makes it look effortless.

Milton Berle (Uncle Miltie) headlined the Embassy's 50th Anniversary show. Appearing with him were the Harmonica Rascals. Buddy Nolan was an added attraction. Newspapers commented:

> As the Grande Page organ rose from the stage's depths, Nolan's smile was as bright as the spotlights on his white tuxedo . . . he gave the audience a taste of his expertise and a good lesson on one of the things the Embassy Theater is all about—the marvelous theater organ.

W. James Bridges
Proudly
Presents

*To The Embassy
Theatre
love!
Red Skelton*

RED SKELTON

*America's
Pantomimist
Extraordinaire*

A Red Skelton–autographed program. *Embassy Theatre Foundation archives*

THE 1980S

The 1980s brought Broadway again to Fort Wayne. The 1981 Embassy season included *Annie,* Bob Fosse's *Dancin'* and *Chorus Line,* and Neil Simon's *They're Playing Our Song.*

Students from Fort Wayne's Whitney Young and Memorial Park magnet schools also appeared on the Embassy stage for a Fine Arts Extravaganza in 1981. Manager Tom Weidemann, who opened the building to the students at no charge, said there are few things more gratifying than seeing children react to the experience of the historic theatre and hearing applause as they perform. Betty Stein, assistant principal at Memorial Park during those years, says this experience was one of the most memorable of her career.

Among the bigger hits of the 1980s were appearances by B.B. King; Peter, Paul, and Mary; Mel Torme; Buddy Rich and his Orchestra; and Henny Youngman. Appearances by Wayne Newton and Perry Como were sell-outs.

THE 1990S

Embassy management continued to reach out to children in the 1990s with stage performances of *Sesame Street Live* and *Teenage Mutant Ninja Turtles.* Both shows drew full houses of squealing, excited children. Adults saw The Statler Brothers, Harry Belafonte, The Fifth Dimension, and Grammy winners Vince Gill and Kathy Mattea, among others.

The Embassy's decision to bring the traveling production of *Hair* to Fort Wayne generated much excitement and was well-attended. Broadway spectaculars such as *Cats, Les Miserables,* and appearances by The Lettermen, Jay Leno, Bill Cosby, and Mel Torme, left audiences rewarded and rejuvenated.

THE 2000S

The Embassy's offerings in the new century continue with more headliners, more variety, and more frequency than ever before. The 2000–2001 season got off to a great start with sold-out houses for both Bill Cosby and Jerry Seinfeld, who as he first walked on the stage and looked at the theatre, could only utter "Wow!"—a typical reaction for many of the performers who marvel at the size and beauty of the auditorium. Audiences also enjoyed the off-the-wall humor of George Carlin as well as an appearance by B.B. King. The year 2002 brought the very popular Ray Romano, fresh from his hit TV series, *Everybody Loves Raymond.* Diane Schuur, Michael Bolton, and Brad Paisley rounded out the year along with one of the frequent appearances of illusionist David Copperfield. The year 2003 marked the observance of the Embassy's 75th anniversary and, to help celebrate the occasion, Willie Nelson, Weird Al Yankovic, Sheryl Crow, and the children's show *Dora the Explorer* all contributed to the year-long festivities. The next season featured Harry Connick Jr., the Moscow Ballet, and Tim Conway and Harvey Korman of the *Carol Burnett TV Show,* bringing down the house with their zany antics.

The Embassy has enjoyed a long affiliation with Jam Theatricals to bring in top Broadway shows. Among the performances in the 2000s were *Stomp, Chicago, Hairspray, Cabaret, Annie Get Your Gun, Lord of the Dance, Grease, Riverdance, Fosse, The King*

The Lettermen. *Embassy Theatre Foundation archives*

and I, and *Rent.* The performances of both *Miss Saigon* and *Mamma Mia!* used eight large trucks to bring in stage sets. In addition to Broadway shows were classic pop and rock stars such as Jethro Tull, The Monkees, Alice Cooper, John Prine, REO Speedwagon, ZZ Top, Lynyrd Skynyrd, and Styx.

Interspersed with all the other theatrical activities, the Fort Wayne Philharmonic, the Embassy's premier tenant, presents its Masterworks and Pops concerts in approximately eighteen performances at the Embassy each year. The Philharmonic orchestra annually features the Philharmonic Chorus as well as guest artists such as Melissa Manchester, Burt Bacharach, Patti Austin, and Wayne Brady on the Embassy stage. These glittering evenings are special events in the Embassy's long list of offerings and showcase the magnificent auditorium at its finest.

After eighty years of operation, the Embassy remains the queen of Indiana theatres. The grand old lady has moved gracefully into the twenty-first century. She continues to welcome audiences and makes every effort to provide Fort Wayne and the surrounding area with the greatest variety of the best of entertainment.

Above. The Fort Wayne Philharmonic performs a Holiday Pops series each December that features the Philharmonic's orchestra and chorus. *Photo courtesy of the Fort Wayne Philharmonic*

Overleaf. Lou Cucinelli of the Fort Wayne band *I, Wombat* performs at the February 9, 2008, Embassy concert, *Down the Line: Legends from Locals.* *Photo by Steve Linsenmayer*

This AAA advertisement promotes
the Hotel Indiana, which also boasted
a drugstore, restaurant, and shops.
Embassy Theatre Foundation archives

THE INDIANA HOTEL

Although a 15' × 40' neon sign clearly identified the building as Hotel Indiana, people have consistently called it the Indiana Hotel. Opening May 24, 1928, the Indiana claimed to provide "the world's best beds" and "furniture as modern as the moment" for its approximate 250 guestrooms, each with private bath. A wrought-iron and glass marquee on Jefferson Boulevard at Harrison Street marked the entry.

Early advertisements touted the hotel as "a desirable stopping place for the traveling public." With small but inexpensive rooms, it was both convenient and comfortable for the vaudeville players who performed at the Emboyd Theatre. It was also handy for salesmen who needed lodging close to the Baker Street train station and the Wabash Railroad station, both only three short blocks away. The hotel even provided a sample room at the end of each hall for salesmen to store their wares. During World War II, officers in the Army Air Corps bunked in the hotel due to lack of available space at Baer Field Airport. A private dining room in the basement known as the Old Fort Room became a makeshift barracks with cots set up for the men who were shipping out.

Bob Goldstine, one of the founders and the first president of the Embassy Theatre Foundation, often told the story about James Keenan and Clyde Quimby, who were friends. Quimby operated theatres and Keenan owned the Keenan Hotel on the corner of Washington Boulevard and Harrison Street. Keenan had an opportunity to lease downtown property he owned to the Lowe's theatre chain. Quimby heard of the negotiations and said, "If my friend is going to compete with me then we had better plan to build a hotel along with the theatre." In time Keenan got out of the theatre deal, but Quimby went ahead with his plans for the hotel.

Austin Cooper III was the first manager and operator of the Indiana Hotel. He was not above occasionally turning on the lights in unoccupied guestrooms along Jefferson and Harrison as a deceptive message to Jim Keenan at the nearby Keenan Hotel that the Indiana was sold out.

Located at the corner of Harrison and Jefferson, the hotel building wraps around the Embassy Theatre in an L shape. It is seven stories tall with two more levels below ground. Exterior walls are faced with Pennsylvania fireclay brick and trimmed with terra cotta. Corinthian columns, small spiral columns, balustrades across the top floor, and a sculpted cornice give it an opulent look.

Facing page and below. An angel and rooftop pineapple grace the terra cotta exterior of the hotel building. *Photos by Ray Soughan; Embassy Theatre Foundation archives*

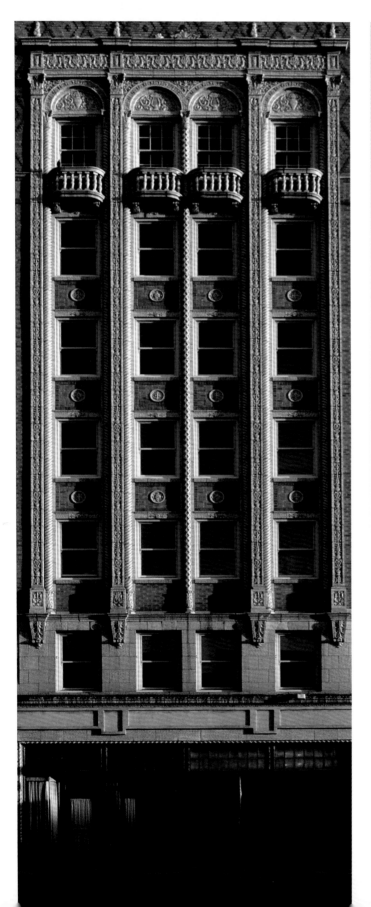

Above. A room number, room rate cards —rooms were $5.50 for one and $7.50 for two guests— and room key fobs remain from the early days of the hotel. *Embassy Theatre Foundation archives*

Below. This sign, "Quiet Please," is today barely visible from its exterior-brick location at the west side of the hotel building. *Embassy Theatre Foundation archives*

Left. A closer look at the north wall of the hotel reveals detailed columns and brick work. *Photo by Steve Linsenmayer*

The lobby is decorated in Spanish revival style and features a mezzanine that surrounds the two-story room. The floor, as well as the risers between steps leading to the mezzanine, contains intricately designed tiles that match well with the marble-topped reception desk, at one time complete with letter boxes that held messages for hotel guests. At various times the lobby included a drugstore, flower shop, saloon, and barbershop. The hotel also operated a restaurant with large windows that faced out onto Jefferson Boulevard as well as a private dining room located on the lower level. Dumbwaiters that extended all the way to the seventh floor carried food and dirty dishes between the basement-level kitchen and the main floor dining room.

In 1945, the Alsonette Hotel Company of Tulsa, Oklahoma, leased Hotel Indiana from Fox Realty Co. and operated it through 1971. Jack Glass, a current volunteer for the Embassy Theatre and bellhop at the hotel in the early 1950s, likes to relate stories about guests of the hotel in those days. He mentions the sweet little old lady who checked

Risers between the steps from the hotel lobby to the mezzanine level contain original and colorful tiles. Stairs to the lower-level restrooms in the theatre also display embedded tiles in the risers. *Photo by Steve Vorderman*

Facing page. The hotel first floor and mezzanine were restored in 1995 and boast the original floor tiles with replica lighting fixtures. The Indiana Hotel is the venue of choice for many business meetings, weddings, and receptions. *Photo by Steve Vorderman*

Above. Scattered among the solid-colored tiles of the hotel lobby floor are etched and glazed drawings of various sizes, depicting a lion, vines, flowers, love birds, and this peacock. *Photo by Steve Vorderman*

into the hotel but was not satisfied with any of the rooms. Jack finally showed her a room on the second floor at the head of the stairs. She said it was perfect. And so it was, because three days later she carried her bag the short distance down the stairs and out the front door to the Greyhound Bus station one half block down the street without paying for her room. The hotel clerk called some contacts in other cities and discovered that she had been doing this all over the country.

Jack also tells the story of two wrestlers who checked in to the hotel in preparation for a highly advertised grudge match that evening at the Allen County Memorial Coliseum. The two met for drinks and dinner in the hotel restaurant, but left for the Coliseum in different taxis. Later that evening, after a wild and furious wrestling match, they returned to the hotel, met in the bar, and drank the rest of the evening, the best of friends to the end.

Although the building including the theatre and the hotel was sold in 1970 to Cinecom Corp., Alsonette continued to lease the hotel. When Cinecom announced the sale of the building in 1971, however, Alsonette closed the hotel. Labor costs and loss of business to motels were factors influencing the decision to sell. During the last month of operation, a hotel staff of twenty-five served fewer than forty guests.

On September 27, 1971, a sale offered furnishings and fixtures to the public. The elevator delivered items from guestrooms to the lobby as fast as they could be sold. Beds went for $8, dressers for $12, and lamps for $3. A sign on an old cash register simply said "Make an Offer."

After the Embassy Theatre Foundation purchased the building in 1975, the hotel served primarily as a storage facility. In 1995, during the theatre's stage renovation, the foundation's board, inspired by the vision and encouragement of Doris Stovall, executive director, decided to renovate the lobby space into a reception hall complete with a catering kitchen and a wet bar. The reception desk was remodeled into a serving bar for patrons. The original lighting, most of which was damaged and beyond repair, was replaced by new light fixtures and chandeliers. The lobby was outfitted with up-to-date, comfortable furniture reminiscent of the style of the building. While guests enjoy modern furnishings and conveniences, touches such as the original mail chute near the elevator doors and the elaborately carved water fountain stand as reminders of the hotel's early days of grandeur.

Below. The first foundation president, Bob Goldstine, with an unidentified female assistant, cuts the ribbon at the re-opening of the Indiana Hotel lobby in 1995. *Embassy Theatre Foundation archives*

Facing page. The hotel lobby water fountain is no longer operable yet remains an important architectural feature. *Photo by Steve Vorderman*

The mezzanine floor of the hotel was converted to offices for the foundation as well as additional banquet space. The floor above the lobby and mezzanine is used for storage and contains old office files, decorations for the Festival of Trees, and various pieces of equipment. The fourth to the seventh floors remain relatively undisturbed since the hotel ceased operations. Several of the rooms still contain original bathroom fixtures and flooring.

Throughout the years the Embassy Theatre Foundation has undertaken many feasibility studies to examine various uses for the top four floors of the hotel, but none ever proved economically sound. However, recent developments associated with the city's Harrison Square project may finally provide a catalyst for change. Harrison Square is a public-private urban redevelopment effort which will occupy several blocks directly west of the Embassy Theatre and Indiana Hotel building. The development will include a baseball stadium, condominiums, retail space, parking garage, and a hotel. A walkway from the new hotel to the Grand Wayne convention center across the street will pass through the building upon completion by 2010. In addition, a stairwell will be added to the east side that will provide access to floors three through seven and an elevator will be installed on the west side of the building that will go from the basement to the seventh floor. It is hoped that better and easier access to the hotel will result in the opportunity for restoration or redevelopment of the hotel space.

When this final piece of the puzzle is complete the Indiana Hotel will continue its traditional role as a downtown gathering place busy with various meetings, dinner parties, receptions, and a variety of activities.

Facing page. Pre-show dining made a dramatic return to the Indiana Hotel in 2008, thanks to a partnership with Joseph Decuis Restaurant of Roanoke. Patrons dined prior to a Broadway at the Embassy performance of *Chicago* on March 13, 2008. *Photo by Patrick Taylor*

The Embassy's grand lobby is radiant with holiday decorations, as families enjoy the annual Festival of Trees. *Photo by Steve Linsenmayer*

5

THE FOUNDATION

The Embassy Theatre Foundation, Inc. is the governing body that oversees the Embassy Theatre and Indiana Hotel. The mission of the foundation is "to restore, preserve and operate Indiana's largest historic theatre; to provide and present quality artistic programs for the cultural enrichment of Greater Fort Wayne and its surrounding area; to provide a facility and performance hall for use by other presenters and civic, arts, educational and service-oriented organizations; and to maintain an image reflecting excellence, innovation and leadership."

A twenty-one-member volunteer board of directors governs the foundation with each director potentially serving two consecutive three-year terms. A paid executive director and staff handle day-to-day operations while the board defines the role of the Embassy in the community, guides the fundraising program, and assures the stated mission is carried out.

The foundation grew out of a desire to preserve not only the building but also the Grande Page organ. In the years of waning movie presentations and during the dark years in the early 1970s when the theatre was closed to the public, a group of organ devotees regularly met with Buddy Nolan, former house organist, on Saturday mornings to keep the pipe organ in playing condition. Included were Bob Goldstine, Robert Nickerson, Dyne Pfeffenberger, Ellsworth Smith, and William Zabel.

This group formed the Embassy Theatre Foundation with Bob Goldstine elected as first president. It was incorporated in late 1972 as a nonprofit, self-perpetuating organization and received tax-exempt status in 1974. The goal of the foundation was to rescue the building and the organ and to operate the theatre as an auditorium for public use.

Of immediate concern to the foundation was a proposal from a group of Indianapolis investors to convert the Indiana Hotel into a housing facility for elderly residents with funding from the U.S. Department of Housing and Urban Development (HUD). Under the plan, the Embassy Theatre would have been demolished to make way for a parking lot and grassy area to service the housing development.

Tax liens, mortgage foreclosures, and layers of corporate owners clouded ownership of the building. In 1952, the Alliance Theatre chain of Chicago had taken over operation of the Emboyd, renaming it the Embassy. In 1968, the Embassy and the Indiana Hotel were sold by the Fox Realty Co. to Arthur T. Gault of Chicago who then sold to S. J. Gregory, president of Alliance Theaters. In 1970, Alliance sold the property to Cinecom Corporation, a distributor of motion pictures, which filed bankruptcy in 1972 causing the theatre to close its doors. Disposition of Cinecom's assets was made by the bankruptcy court in New York City. It was this court that gave authorization to the Embassy Theatre Foundation to use the theatre for $1 a month, cancelable on 30 days notice, making it possible for the foundation to begin cleaning the theatre and preparing it for various events.

Scores of foundation members contributed time, talent, and funds. They filled Dumpsters with debris, cleaned, scrubbed, and painted surfaces and fixtures. They scraped grease off concession equipment that had been used during the movie theatre days. They removed coal dust from the carpeting and seat upholstery. The Indiana Hotel, once designated as a bomb shelter, was cleared of five-gallon drums filled with water and the emptied containers were then used as trash cans.

Facing page. In October 1952, new owner Alliance Theatre held its opening night of the renamed Embassy Theatre.
Embassy Theatre Foundation archives

Above. In the mid-1970s, volunteers participated in countless work sessions such as this one in order to prepare the Embassy for eventual reopening. *Embassy Theatre Foundation archives*

During this time the foundation scheduled several productions. On March 10, 1974, Colonel John D. Craig, recipient of awards for both his military efforts and expert undersea exploration, presented a benefit film, *The Mysterious Sea.* More than 650 people paid $1.50 each to see the work of the first filmmaker to produce underwater movies in color. Colonel Craig donated his time and effort to the Embassy in exchange for his "staying over" expenses.

On March 16, Columbia duo harpists Longstreet and Escosa, both native Hoosiers, performed a benefit concert that netted $1,000 for the foundation. Then, on April 1, Robert O'Reilly, a professional photographer from Fort Wayne, presented *Alluring Australia,* a well-received travelogue.

In March 1974, however, the bankruptcy court in New York City awarded the Embassy property to Solarsystems, Inc., one of the largest creditors of Cinecom Corp. Solarsystems gave notice to the Embassy Theatre Foundation to vacate the property on April 30, 1974. The mortgage holder on the Embassy property at this time was Montgomery Ward Company. Cinecom's payments to Montgomery Ward were one year in arrears

Donors and volunteers wore badges to promote the Embassy and fundraising campaigns, such as the first one in the 1970s, top, and later in 1984. *Embassy Theatre Foundation archives*

so Montgomery Ward filed a foreclosure suit in Allen County, Indiana, court against Sportservice Company, a company that managed concession services at many of the country's large sporting venues, which had acquired title to the Embassy from Solarsystems. Fred Hunter, a local real estate manager serving as the court-appointed receiver for the Embassy property, allowed the Embassy Theatre Foundation to re-enter the property to resume its custodial functions.

Also, early in 1974, the federal government withdrew its promise for HUD funding for the conversion of the hotel to a home for elderly and the subsequent demolition of the theatre. Consequently, the Indianapolis investors opted not to purchase the property, clearing the way for the Embassy Theatre Foundation to step in as a potential buyer.

The foundation began to measure the community's interest in raising funds to purchase the theatre. It circulated petitions and sponsored open houses on two successive weekends. Each brought hundreds of people from the Fort Wayne area, eager to see the theatre's interior. Foundation members and volunteers acted as tour guides, ticket sellers, and membership recruiters. Despite inclement weather during one of the weekends, the foundation realized $4,300 in dues and contributions.

It was Bob Goldstine who worked to keep communication lines open with Montgomery Ward and Sportservice Company during this rocky period of negotiations. Finally, on August 28, 1974, the foundation signed an agreement with Sportservice Company to purchase the Embassy Theatre and Indiana Hotel property. Although the replacement value of the building was determined to be $15 million, Sportservice Company wanted to use the transaction as a tax contribution deduction, so the sale price was set at $250,000—provided the foundation could raise the money within sixty days.

Organ crew chief Byron Fogt, holding a flashlight, leads
a tour of the stage as part of an effort to educate the
community and raise funds to purchase the building.
Used with permission of the Fort Wayne News-Sentinel

Gasoline Alley, penned by Dick Moores, spotlighted
the Embassy's troubles in a fifty-one-strip series,
bringing national attention to the Embassy's fundraising campaign. © *Tribune Media Services, Inc. All
rights reserved. Reprinted with permission*

Goldstine appealed to the several hundred foundation members to increase their contributions. Kappa Kappa Kappa, a women's organization, donated proceeds from its fashion show and the media charged in with a Save the Embassy campaign. Dick Moores, a Fort Wayne native and writer of the cartoon strip *Gasoline Alley,* picked up the campaign and included the Embassy story in a series of syndicated cartoons running in most of the nation's newspapers in 1975. According to a 1975 article about the cartoon series by *News-Sentinel* reporter Connie Trexler, "Moores said he was the first doorman at the theatre when it opened as the Emboyd in 1928. . . . He said he was promoted to assistant manager, in charge of the theatre from 5 to 7 PM 'when nothing happened.'"

Volunteers set up kiosks in both Glenbrook and Southtown shopping centers. They distributed pamphlets, answered questions about the theatre, and sold memberships to the Embassy Theatre Foundation. During this time many automobiles in the Fort Wayne area sported bumper stickers claiming, "I Gave to Save the Embassy." The foundation received donations from more than twenty-five hundred donors.

A huge block of Wisconsin cheese was purchased from Hickory Farms Co. and shipped to the theatre. It was set up in the theatre lobby and foundation members at various Embassy events sold pieces of cheese for $1.

One of the more creative fundraising tactics was the sale of slices of cheese from a two-ton barrel. *Embassy Theatre Foundation archives*

The foundation also hired Ketchum Inc., a professional fundraising firm, to determine feasibility to generate the sale price and an additional equal amount to replace the roof and heating and air conditioning systems. Ketchum determined there was a possibility the foundation could raise the necessary funds with a "properly organized campaign." It recommended soliciting 40 percent of the goal from corporate and individual contributors before appealing to the general public. Essential to success was the need to obtain a six-month extension on the contract deadline. Goldstine received the extension on November 5.

It was December 2, 1974, when the foundation made the initial down payment of $10,000. The balance was due on June 2, 1975. The fundraising campaign guided by Ketchum was a resounding success and the foundation was able to pay the $240,000 balance in the spring of 1975. With that transaction completed, the foundation realized its goal of saving the building and the Page pipe organ.

Since those early days, the foundation has not only operated the facility on a day-to-day basis but also constantly worked to improve the theatre and hotel. In 1980 all of the seats were removed and new seats and upholstery were installed. The seats on the main floor also were repositioned with a wider space between rows so that patrons could enjoy

Above. Everyone closely followed the foundation's efforts to save the Embassy, including local news media. *Reprinted with permission of* The Journal Gazette, *Fort Wayne, Indiana*

Facing page, top. Volunteers stripped the theatre's main floor of its seats in preparation for frame repairs and cushion replacements. *Photo by Ray Soughan; Embassy Theatre Foundation archives*

Facing page, bottom. Scaffolding reaches up to the very top of the theatre dome so that repairs to the plaster and ornate paint could be made. *Photo by Ray Soughan; Embassy Theatre Foundation archives*

more leg room. A new main curtain was purchased for $22,000 and in 1990 a new lambrequin, the drapery at the top of the stage archway, was installed to recapture as much as possible the original appearance of the proscenium.

In the mid-1990s, the foundation undertook the most extensive renovation of the theatre yet, with a major expansion of the stage and orchestra pit, resulting in a house that can now accommodate almost any touring theatrical company.

In 2005, the foundation acquired a new, state-of-the-art marquee and blade, or vertical, sign. The marquee with its digital sign boards is able to display messages about Embassy events in a variety of colors and designs, all programmed from a computer. The three-story-high blade sign displays in large letters "Embassy" and is reminiscent of the original vertical sign announcing the location of the Emboyd Theatre. Along with the new signage, the foundation, in cooperation with the City of Fort Wayne, designed and built a new sidewalk the length of the building, which features bricks of varying sizes with names and messages of donors. Interspersed among the bricks are diamond-shaped brass plaques which name national personalities that hail from Fort Wayne. The names of people such as Herb Shriner, Carole Lombard, and Shelley Long are included in the sidewalk.

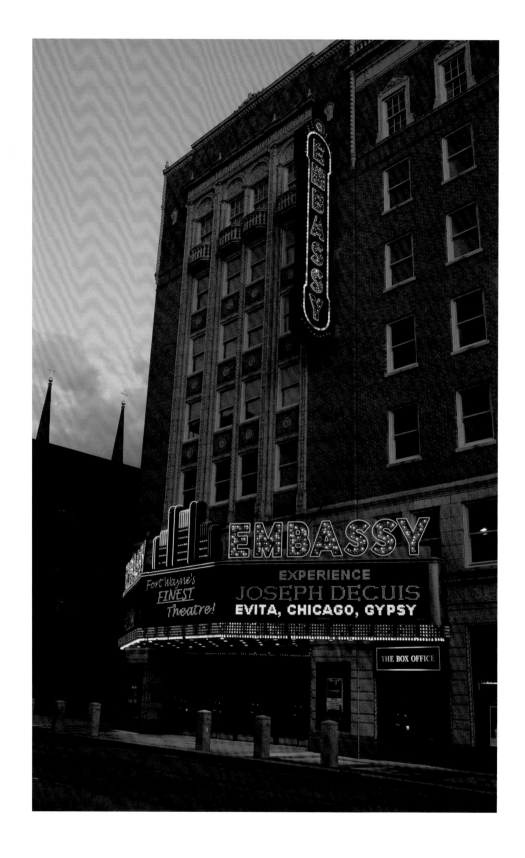

Throughout these years of accomplishment one group of volunteers has had an important and special relationship to the Embassy. The Embassadors, sometimes known as the Angels of the Embassy, was established in 1981 as a group of volunteers to organize fundraising events. Board member Marge Irmscher coordinated the first meeting and encouraged her friends to become involved with the ongoing restoration of the theatre. At the first meeting, Pat Kunkel was elected president and the group adopted its name. In subsequent meetings the structure of the organization was established and its mission was determined by its members. The first of its many fundraising activities was handling the wine sales at special Embassy events. In the first two years alone, $3,000 was raised, which the foundation used for the initial restoration of the lobby concession area.

Then in 1983, Barbara Wigham, program director for WPTA-TV and member of the Embassadors, visited Erie, Pennsylvania, and attended a Festival of Trees event as a fundraiser for a local hospital. She brought the idea back to Fort Wayne, and the next year Mary Lane and Mary Ellen Rice, representing the Embassadors and the Embassy Theatre Foundation, traveled to Erie to attend the festival. They immediately knew this was the kind of fundraiser that would be successful for the Embassy, and so the Embassadors began to organize for a similar event at the Embassy.

The first Festival of Trees took place in 1985. It consisted of scores of professionally decorated Christmas trees strategically placed for viewing throughout the theatre. That first festival provided enough proceeds to enable the theatre to replace the aging front doors. With the success of the first venture, the Embassadors committed to offering the Festival of Trees annually.

In each of the ensuing years tens of thousands of people have attended the festival to view the lavishly decorated trees, to visit with Santa Claus, to browse through the Christmas shop, and to enjoy various entertainment groups performing on stage. For many, the annual Festival of Trees is a family event that marks the beginning of the holiday season.

The Embassadors, with its many dedicated volunteers, was crucial to the theatre in its efforts to update and maintain the facility. The Embassadors raised well over a half million dollars and enabled the Embassy Theatre Foundation to undertake improvements such as installation of handicapped restrooms, renovation of dressing rooms, relocation of the box office, and many other upgrades and enhancements of the complex's facilities. In 2000, the Embassadors disbanded as a formal organization. However, many of its dedicated volunteers continue to devote time and energies to the Festival of Trees, ushering duties, and other activities in support of the Embassy.

There are a number of historic theatres located throughout the country, with many owned and operated by a governmental unit, such as a city or county agency. The Embassy, however, is one of the few historic theatres that is owned and operated by a nonprofit foundation. As a result, the foundation has always been able to react more quickly and responsively to community input. For example, some years ago the board of directors

Facing page. Today's blade sign towers over the marquee, which features three computerized message boards; both were installed for the Embassy's seventy-fifth birthday. *Photo by Steve Linsenmayer*

decided to promote its own theatrical shows and presentations. It was quickly discovered, however, that this involved risk which put the foundation in a perilous financial condition. The board was quickly able to revert back to being a rental house. Today, almost all of the shows at the Embassy are brought in by promoters who rent the theatre and its services. As a result, the foundation today enjoys a sound financial footing without having to assume the risk inherent in promoting shows.

Nonetheless, the Embassy does produce some of its shows, especially those which reflect community interest or talent. The Grande Page pipe organ plays such an important part in the history of the theatre that, in its desire to spotlight the instrument, the Embassy sponsors at least two organ concerts each season featuring worldclass theatre organists. Also, the foundation has always felt it important to showcase local talent. The annual Festival of Trees has many local groups perform on stage during the festival. The popular series entitled *Down the Line: Legends from Locals* is sponsored by the Embassy and is a collaborative effort with local media, ad agencies, various businesses, and local bands to emulate rock music legends. Members of the bands consider it an honor to perform at the Embassy and large audiences love seeing their friends on stage.

The theatre plays host to a number of non-theatrical events, such as social occasions, high school graduations, the Indiana State Bodybuilders Championships, and the Sterling Sentinel Awards event sponsored by Fort Wayne Newspapers. Of course, the theatre also on occasion shows vintage films on northeastern Indiana's largest movie screen.

Facing page. Nearly fifteen thousand people each year visit the Festival of Trees, with fifty trees decorated by local designers and organizations displayed throughout the theatre and hotel. *Photo by Steve Linsenmayer*

Left. An unidentified patron purchases a ticket at the theatre box office. *Photo by Patrick Taylor*

Concert-goers can now print their own tickets, which
are scanned at the entrance, here by volunteer usher Richard
Ruthsatz. *Photo by Patrick Taylor*

The direction provided and the progress achieved by the Embassy Theatre Foundation
in the past thirty-five years have resulted in a first-rate performance and meeting facility with a national reputation. The theatre averages more than 125,000 patrons enjoying
close to a hundred performances every year. Including rehearsal times and lobby events,
the theatre is booked more than two hundred nights a year, including every weekend
from June through August when the hotel and theatre lobbies are booked for weddings
and receptions. The theatre and the enjoyment it has brought to the community have far
exceeded the dreams of the six original founders. None of these accomplishments would
have been possible without the hard work and dedication of talented board, staff, and
foundation members, hundreds of loyal volunteers, and thousands of concerned Fort
Wayne area citizens, who refused to lose an irreplaceable community treasure.

As part of the Festival of Trees and downtown HolidayFest activities, the Embassy sets electric candles in each of the hotel's west-side windows. *Photo by Steve Linsenmayer*

This drawing of Bud Berger was
used in a local newspaper feature
article in the 1970s and is displayed
in the main hallway of the Embassy
administrative offices. *Embassy
Theatre Foundation archives*

THE PEOPLE

The Embassy Theatre and Indiana Hotel complex is a notable and architectural treasure for Fort Wayne. However, as in most organizations, the people that are involved and the synergy that exists between the building and the people who worked so diligently to save and operate it make for some of the most interesting stories. This book would be incomplete without a salute to the many people who made a powerful and lasting impact upon this beautiful theatre. It is their enthusiasm for, support of, and dedication to this grand palace that is the true heart of the Embassy. This chapter is dedicated to all of these people and to the audiences, past and present, who have filled the house with so many magical memories. Here are just a few of their stories.

Bud Berger, stage manager of the Embassy from 1936 until his death in 1965, worked with all the vaudeville players, acrobats, big band musicians, organists, and lone performers that appeared at the Embassy. He gave big helpings of Hoosier hospitality to the greats and wannabes alike. It was Bud who provided neckties to forgetful performers, built last-minute props, ironed shirts, and played rounds of gin rummy and poker with all.

Many of the performers wrote personal messages on their photographs for Bud. Among them are the following:

The Smoothies, 1942: *Bud—We appreciate everything that you've done for us. We never had a person look after us as much as you. Thanking you again.*

Clyde McCoy and the Bennett Sisters, 1942: . . . *You made our engagement a real pleasure.*

Cab Calloway, 1945: *To Bud—The grandest guy there is—Lots of Luck.*

Bud lived in a backstage room, now the green room, for many years. There he watched over the theatre and lavished his love and attention on it. Because Bud had no family in the area, the Embassy and its employees became his family. It was Bud's final and fulfilled wish that he be cremated and his ashes scattered on the Embassy roof.

Present-day volunteers and employees claim that Bud's spirit is still present in the theatre. Fort Wayne *News-Sentinel* writer Thomas Zaenger included the following story in a feature article written about Bud in 1978, the Embassy's 50th anniversary year:

A lone Embassy volunteer sits at the Page organ late one night. The theater is empty. The volunteer stretches his fingers toward the keys. A squeaking and groaning of a seat being sat in is heard in the darkness. The organist turns and sees that one aisle seat is down. He plays for a half hour, all the while feeling a presence in the theater. When he finishes his "concert," he hears the sound of a seat again . . . he turns and looks . . . the seat on the aisle is up. The spirit of Bud has enjoyed another concert.

———— ⚬⚬⚬ ————

Becky Sumpter became acquainted with the theatre in 1973. She was president of the Adena Carney Women's Club, and the members decided to help the Embassy Theatre volunteers in their efforts to purchase the theatre. The foundation board had grown to fifteen members and named Sumpter its recording secretary. For the next fifteen years she was among the growing band of volunteers committed to saving the theatre.

"Once the auditorium and stage were usable," she recalled, "we brought in anybody who would do anything for free." There were vaudeville acts including comedian Henny Youngman and vocalist Crystal Gayle. The legendary Bob Hope gave a benefit concert and told Sumpter afterward, "Thank you for saving my theatre."

"We made good friends—life-long friends who became more like family than our real family," Sumpter said. "Labor Day clean-up became one of our traditions. Because there was no air conditioning, the Embassy locked its doors during the summer. Labor Day weekend we got the place ready for the fall season. After the work, adults and children shared potluck meals and went onstage to dance and sing to the organ and piano music."

———— ⚬⚬⚬ ————

Dorothy Eichman relates the story of how her father met her mother, a young lady appearing at the Embassy Theatre in the 1930s show *Hellzapoppin*. While attending a performance, Ray Racine noticed an attractive young chorine on stage and, after the show, asked her out for a cup of coffee. She accepted and the two hit it off right away. After many letters and telephone calls, their relationship blossomed and eventually Ray convinced the object of his affection to give up show business and settle down in Fort Wayne. Ray eventually became a stagehand at the Embassy and worked many shows at the theatre where he met his wife. And, in the 1960s, their daughter, Dorothy, served as box office manager.

From his first appearance in 1928, Bob Hope remained a big fan of the Embassy stage. *Embassy Theatre Foundation archives*

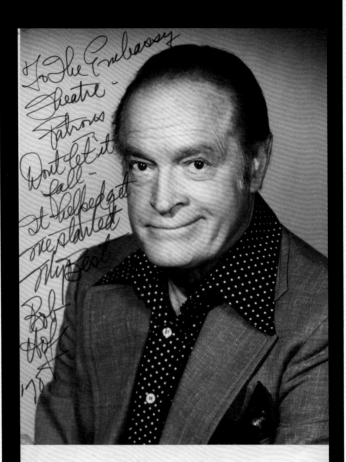

BOB HOPE

April 23, 1975

Mrs. Mildred E. Finrow
3229 So. Clinton Street
Fort Wayne, Indiana 46806

Dear Mrs. Finrow:

Thank youfor your letter. It saddens me to learn that the Emboyd Theatre may hit the skids. It played a big part in my earlier days when I needed food. It is a beautiful place and I remember introducing Fred Allen one time, he walked out with a wheelbarrow, took out a banjo as though he was going to play, then put it back and walked off the stage.

I sure wish I could make the golf tournament but I am scheduled to do another show at that time, so I must forego the pleasure.

I hope and pray the Embassy can be saved.

Regards,

BOB HOPE

Gene Witte attended an open house fundraiser on a cold December afternoon in 1974 that turned into a twenty-year commitment to the Embassy.

In the early days, Witte served as chairman of the facilities committee. He said he had the authority to "fix everything without spending money."

Witte remembers foundation board members had to bring their own chairs to meetings or be forced to stand. In fact, funds were so limited that volunteers often even provided their own cleaning supplies and basic tools.

Local companies donated raw materials as well as professional help. Youth groups including the Future Farmers of America, Boy Scouts, and Girl Scouts cleaned out debris from the large heating and cooling airways under the main auditorium floor. "People bent over backwards for us," Witte said. "Everyone wanted to save the Embassy."

Some of the repairs included painting and re-plastering the auditorium, replacing and reweaving the carpet, and replacing the terra cotta roof trim. Under Witte's supervision, the volunteer corps ripped up the stage floor and tore out the footlights to allow for the professional installation of a sprung floor and modern lighting.

"I went through the blueprints until I LIVED this building," Witte said.

Volunteer Gene Witte makes repairs in the Embassy's gallery, or third-floor, level. *Embassy Theatre Foundation archives*

In the early 1990s, Doris Stovall had just retired from the Pasadena, California, Civic Theatre. She had experienced one earthquake too many and decided to move back to her hometown of Atlanta, Georgia. Once there, however, she discovered she wasn't quite ready for the retirement lifestyle and in early 1992 responded to an ad for executive director of the Embassy Theatre Foundation. She recalled that as she was traveling to Fort Wayne she asked herself, "What on earth am I doing—I can't stand cold weather and I have no warm clothes!" However, upon arrival and one look at the magnificent old theatre, she was sold and decided then and there to accept the position.

She had hanging in her office a large picture of a frog sitting on a lily pad with the caption, "This is my auditorium, and don't you forget it!" The picture had been given to her by her colleagues in Pasadena. One of the Embassy board members came in one day and, noting the picture, informed Doris that the auditorium wasn't "her" auditorium—it was "our" auditorium. Doris was impressed with the sentiment because she felt it reflected the support and pride the community had in the Embassy.

Doris spearheaded the major renovation project in the mid-1990s. She had a dream of enlarging the stage so that it could accommodate any traveling show that came to town. She recalls the rather shocked look on the face of a representative from Martin Company of Fort Wayne when she told him she wanted all seven floors of hotel rooms on the west side of the building torn out. Doris thought on a grand scale, and in her mind she could see the back wall of the stage being moved into the space occupied by the hotel rooms. The Embassy foundation board agreed with Doris's vision and undertook a $5 million capital improvement campaign. And, as they always had in the past, the community generously responded. When the project was completed, not only did the Embassy have a new and much larger stage and orchestra lift, patrons also had more leg room between seat rows, new and brighter lighting in the grand lobby with a freshly painted ceiling, and a newly refurbished and re-designed hotel lobby that could accommodate gatherings for hundreds of people.

After the renovation was finished, Doris was fond of telling people she was familiar with historic theatres from coast to coast and that the Embassy could rival the best of them. However, she again began thinking of returning to Atlanta where her family lived and she could be warm. She left the theatre in June 1999, knowing she was joining a group of former executive directors such as Tom Weidemann and Joan Leal who distinguished themselves in their service to the theatre. Doris was confident and proud of her contribution and knew the Embassy would continue to serve the entertainment needs of northeastern Indiana for many years to come.

Fred and Florence Hitzemann exemplify the wonderful volunteer spirit of Fort Wayne–area citizens. They attended movies at the Embassy as a young couple and, when it appeared the theatre might be torn down, they decided they simply could not allow that to happen. In early 1974, Fred and Florence attended the first open house sponsored by the Embassy foundation and immediately signed up as volunteers. Fred said they would do anything to help save the theatre, although at the time he and Florence never

Doris Stovall, executive director from 1992 to 1999, poses with Charlie Dailey, who is wearing his 1928 usher uniform, at the Embassy's sixty-fifth birthday celebration on May 14, 1993. *Embassy Theatre Foundation archives*

imagined all that promise would eventually entail. They were put on the cleaning detail and brought their own cleaning supplies since the Embassy had none. On many occasions, they would spend the day cleaning only to return at night to help usher and sell concessions. Fred said, "I knew that if the theatre was clean, then people would be more inclined to give to the foundation." One evening, Helene Foellinger, a well-known Fort Wayne philanthropist and one of the Embassy foundation's early donors, asked to meet whoever was cleaning the theatre. She wanted to thank Fred for her feet not sticking to the floor any more.

Throughout the years, Fred and Florence have remained loyal to the theatre and have performed every volunteer job for which the foundation has had a need. Even today, at most performances, one can find Fred taking tickets and Florence ushering. They are now both in their 80s but they still retain their love for and dedication to the theatre. In 2005, the Embassy foundation honored them for more than thirty years of continuous service and named them Embassy Volunteers of the Year. And, just as they started out, they accepted the award together.

Florence and Fred Hitzemann.
Photo by Steve Linsenmayer

⸻⸻

Tom Skiba is a numbers guy. He claims he doesn't have the creativity and artistic originality that some of his fellow board members do, but he can tally up and balance columns of figures with the best of them.

Tom is a CPA and a partner in the accounting firm Haines Isenbarger & Skiba. He has served on the Embassy foundation board since 1992 with only one or two short absences. He has been the treasurer of the foundation during many of those years, and even served as president during the tumultuous days of the mid-1990s when the Embassy foundation undertook a major renovation of the stage and hotel lobby. Tom recalls standing next to Doris Stovall, then the executive director, looking at a huge mud hole that was inhabiting the spacewhere the Embassy stage was once located and saying to Doris, "This better work or we're dead!"

He had good reason to be apprehensive. In just a few days, seven floors of hotel rooms and retail space were to be blasted away from the center of a building that was already almost seventy years old. The community had pledged more than $5 million for the project and was expecting all to go as planned. And it did. The rooms were removed without the building falling in on itself, the stage was expanded to accommodate any traveling show, and the hotel lobby was modified so that it can easily handle meetings of hundreds of people.

Tom states, "I view the Embassy as yet one more tool in the city's effort toward economic development—an important community asset that helps reflect the quality of life in Fort Wayne that is so important to companies considering relocating to northeastern Indiana." Operating the theatre in a prudent and fiscally responsible manner, tending to ever-present repairs in a historic building, and providing quality and diverse entertainment are responsibilities Tom and other board members take very seriously.

Tom Skiba. *Photo courtesy of Tom Skiba*

Tom is particularly pleased that the foundation has an endowment that exceeds $650,000. He says, "This reflects the community's confidence in the many talented and dedicated individuals who over the years have served on the Embassy foundation board." Tom may not believe he has creativity and artistic originality but he certainly does share the vision and commitment that so exemplifies other board members. And we are indeed glad that he is a "numbers guy."

As the eleventh executive director of the Embassy Theatre Foundation, Kelly Updike is one of the many Fort Wayne natives who understand the building's place in history.

"People constantly ask me why the Embassy is so valued by the community," Kelly says, "and the reason is pretty simple: It was built with love and it was rescued by regular folks who had that same passion.

"This building was built by smart business leaders who used the best artisans and materials possible; it has a strong foundation. That same enduring emotion keeps the Embassy in the hearts of the community; the people of Fort Wayne love the treasure they almost lost to a wrecking ball."

Kelly isn't shy when it comes to comparing other theatres to the Embassy. "Many buildings are awe-inspiring but few surpass our warmth and ornate beauty," she stated. "However, we are more than just a pretty face. By helping today's young people create their own memories in the Embassy, we are instilling the same passion that will sustain the Embassy for generations to come."

To that end, it is important to preserve the Embassy while presenting programs that are innovative and current with today's standards. The Embassy honors its heritage by producing annual Pops on Pipes organ concerts, a silent movie with organ accompaniment, and open-console events led by organ-club enthusiasts. The Embassy also offers star performers and new events, such as a rock show featuring local bands and educational performances for schoolchildren.

"There are several consistent themes through the Embassy's decades," Kelly said. "The maintenance work done in the building fifty and even eighty years ago mirrors the same types of tasks we do today. The performances on the stage remain the same in that, although the headliners change, they are diverse and reach a wide variety of audiences. And, while the faces are different, the people who care for the building are strong and committed to their mission."

Creativity will keep the Embassy alive well past its hundredth birthday. A good example of this is a project that will, by 2010, connect the Embassy via a sky bridge to a new downtown Fort Wayne development called Harrison Square. The complex includes a hotel, parking garage, and baseball park. The sky bridge will connect to the third floor of the Indiana Hotel and pedestrians will be able to walk along that floor to another sky bridge to the Grand Wayne Center. The project provides opportunity for development of the four floors in the Indiana Hotel that have remained closed for more than thirty years. The walkway will not disturb the historic and decorative terra cotta, a key exterior feature which is important to the Embassy's placement on the National Register of Historic Places.

"We are essentially building bridges on our community's strengths in order to enhance our historic landmark and give it new life," Kelly stated. "It is our intention to honor our founders by involving the community in the dreaming, planning, and building of the walkway and development of the upper floors. The Embassy will continue to shine brightly in downtown Fort Wayne as an active and vibrant gem."

From its opening night as the Emboyd Theatre to its current neon displays, the Embassy has enjoyed a colorful history. *Image above from the Embassy Theatre Foundation archives; photo at right by Steve Linsenmayer*

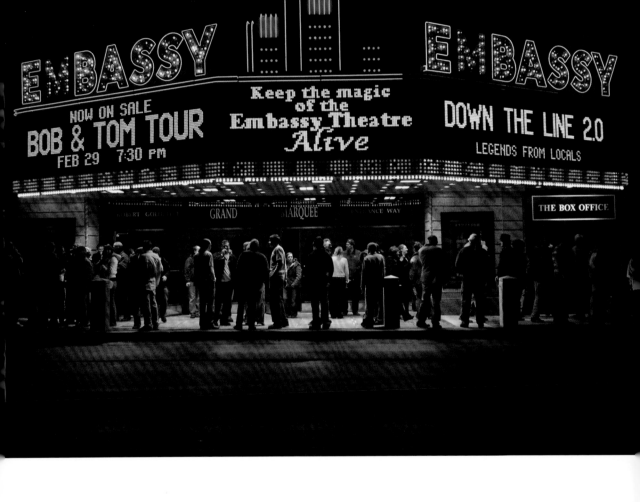

Dyne L. Pfeffenberger is a retired professor of accounting at Indiana University–Purdue University Fort Wayne and an original member of the organization that formed to save and restore the theatre. He is currently the historian for the Embassy Theatre, and plays the organ and piano at Embassy functions, as he has done since 1956.

Marlyn E. Koons is an instructor of composition at Indiana University–Purdue University Fort Wayne.

Kathleen E. Skiba has worked as a deputy city attorney for the City of South Bend and wrote children's book reviews for the *South Bend Tribune*. She is a member of the Illinois State Bar Association, Indiana State Bar Association, and the Allen County Bar Association.